Enough is Enough
*Healing Loudly So Others
Know They Can Heal Too*

Marisa Mason

Enough is Enough

*Healing Loudly So Others
Know They Can Heal Too*

Marisa Mason

Enough is Enough: Healing Loudly So Others Know They Can Heal Too

Copyright © 2025 by Marisa Mason

No part of this book may be reproduced or transmitted in any form or by any means, electronic or mechanical, including photocopy, recording, or any information storage and retrieval system, without the author's prior written permission.

All Bible quotations are taken from the **King James Version (KJV)** unless otherwise stated. All definitions are from the Merriam-Webster Dictionary, unless otherwise noted.

Editor | Var Kelly
Just Write It Services (JWIS), LLC
Email: Info@JustWriteItServices.com |
www.JustWriteItServices.com

Dedication

I dedicate this book to both of my grandmothers. One kept me rooted in The Bible through weekly Bible study, and the other kept me rooted in the physical church building almost every day of the week. Both were under the assignment and will of God in preparing me for my future. While I couldn't understand it at the time, they were leading me to where God wanted me to be — my ultimate destiny.

You are both gone now, but I appreciate you giving me roots and fulfilling The Word of God: *"Train up a child in the way he should go, and when he is old, he will not depart from it."* (Proverbs 22:6)

I also dedicate this book to my children and my grandchildren. I pray that the lessons I had to learn and the brokenness you were raised through keep you from going down the same roads and paths that I have taken. While in my brokenness, I gained strength, it came at a price that, many times, caused you pain as well.

I thank you for being patient with me.

I thank you for not giving up on me.

I thank you for loving me through my bitterness, through my anger, through my brokenness, and through our separation.

I have learned that it is through pain that we grow and birth out our experiences. I am confident in this one thing: the God that we serve will always keep you and protect you, because He is faithful.

Table of Contents

Dedication

Introduction

Chapter 1. Innocence Lost

Chapter 2. Identify Crisis

Chapter 3. Unchosen But Not Unclaimed

Chapter 4. Trapped in the Cycle

Chapter 5. Open Doors

Chapter 6. The Great Escape

Chapter 7. Rebuilding from Ruins

Chapter 8. Finding My Faith

Chapter 9. When Trauma Tries Again

Chapter 10. God at Work– And It's Showing

Chapter 11. A Work in Progress

Chapter 12. Choosing God

About The Author

Stay Connected

Introduction

I wasn't supposed to survive—not with my mind, not with my heart, and certainly not with my faith. I wasn't supposed to make it to the other side of trauma, betrayal, neglect, and shame. But here I am.

If you're holding this book, I believe it's because you've also reached a breaking point. Maybe you've whispered those exact words—*enough is enough*—in the middle of a breakdown, a hospital room, a courtroom, or a silent car ride home. Maybe you said it when they walked away, when the bills piled up, or when you looked in the mirror and didn't recognize who you were anymore. If so, this book is for you.

I wrote this book to tell the truth. To show what it looks like to heal loudly after surviving silently. I didn't grow up with excellent safety, stability, or spiritual guidance. I grew up searching for love and belonging in all the wrong places, picking up pieces of myself after every disappointment. I became a mother while still a child inside. I dragged my children through my pain. I made mistakes. But I also made it out.

This book is not just a story of trauma—it's a story of transformation. It's not polished, and it's not pretty. But it's honest. Every chapter in this book is a marker of God's hand in my life, even when I couldn't see Him. You'll read about dysfunction I normalized, relationships I idolized, and wounds I tried to hide. You'll also read about how God met me in my darkest moments—not always with immediate miracles, but with mercy that rewrote my story.

The phrase *enough is enough* wasn't just something I said—it became a war cry. It was the moment I stopped agreeing with the enemy and began to agree with God. I decided I wouldn't pass my pain down to my children. I chose to heal, to grow, and to say yes to the process of becoming whole. I didn't do this just for myself, but for my children and the generations to come.

So here's my invitation to you: Walk with me through these pages. You won't just read about my battles—you'll find your freedom in them. You might cry. You might pause. You might even feel exposed. That's okay. Healing isn't always clean, but it is always worth it.

This book isn't the end of my story. It's a continuation of God's grace. And if He did it for me, He can do it for you, too.

Chapter 1:
Innocence Lost

It is absolutely amazing how much information our minds can hold, and it is equally impressive, whether good or bad, how much impact a person or persons can have on children from a very young age. I look at my grandchildren today in their tender ages, from birth until preteen, and I wonder how much of life they have already stored in their tender little heads and what impact the little experiences have had on them thus far.

My memories did not seem to have a balance when I began writing this book. I wrote the first version of this book out of my pain and out of a lack of understanding. I realized I needed a release, and writing provided a means to achieve it. The first version of this book allowed me to release the pain, the confusion, and the trauma on paper over 10 years ago. While I thought that was all there was to the book, I am here to say that that was only the beginning. I wrote the book from my perspective on life, as well as my own experiences and situation.

Today, I present to you a new being in Christ Jesus, walking in wisdom, knowledge, and understanding, to share my story from that perspective in hopes of reaching someone else who needs to break free from the enemy's lies.

For as long as I can remember, I grew up in the city of New Jersey. I was about 5 or 6 years old during that time, and I remember participating in small activities, such as visiting the park and spending time with my family. There were always my siblings, whom I do not remember playing with much because they were so young. There were aunts and older cousins. I also remember my uncle; he was the only one there.

I remember my uncle practicing his karate moves in the house for as long as I can remember. I don't know if he was living with us or just visiting, but I do remember him rescuing me from a fire and hurting himself. I remember being in the bathtub and him coming into the bathroom to take me out. Everything happened so fast, but he wrapped me up and jumped out the window with me in his arms. I honestly cannot say that I was afraid or shaken up, but I remember him having to get treatment for his leg and foot.

Today, I am grateful for him; he is one of my favorite Uncles. I am close to him today, and if I had to contribute that closeness to anything, I would say that the fire event was the starting point. I am not sure what came after that incident, but I know we moved to a new residence, and that is where I believe my life began to change.

At this new residence, I recall standing on the kitchen chair with the back of the chair leaning against the sink and my little feet resting on the chair's center, making imprints as I learned to wash dishes. As I write this, I remember that day as if it were yesterday. The light was bright, and we had those old white sinks with two sides. One side had the little engrafted rolls; the water would trickle down in the sink if you set wet dishes there. We had a dish rack on the side, sitting right on top of those rolls.

If I had to guess, I would say I was about five or six years old. I would hear my uncle's voice while he was close, saying, "The forks and knives are turned in so you don't stick yourself." I was a big girl in my eyes, doing grown-up things. It's funny because I have memories of always doing what I was told to do, and not many of doing what I should have.

My sister, three brothers, and I lived in that home with another brother on the way. We had a two-bedroom apartment with a living room and kitchen, and all of us, except my mother and her boyfriend, slept in one bedroom. I was the oldest child in the home at the time, and the most active, because I was constantly being spanked or punished.

What's missing is when my mother's boyfriend came into the picture and when my uncle left. Those memories are nowhere to be found.

We lived next door to my aunt and cousins in this new residence.

My maternal grandmother was my primary caretaker at the time, as I was around the age of 5 or 6. I remember always having to go to her house and stay with her while my little siblings stayed behind.

Another key thing I remember is that whenever I got in trouble, I always had a smile on my face, even when someone spoke to me or disciplined me. I remember my grandmother saying seriously, "Stop smiling because it's not funny, and I am not playing." Little did she know (and neither did I know) that the smile just couldn't be helped. I know today it's called the "nervous" smile.

Days at Grandma's house were always fun. She was a Jehovah's Witness, and she is deceased now, but she was faithful about studying God's Word. I would go with her to people's homes for Bible study and then to the Kingdom Hall for service. At her house, she would cook or clean; meanwhile, my youngest uncle would handcuff me to the chair as a joke, but I hated it.

He was a real jokester, I have to say. He always did things as a joke and never as abuse. It was all in good fun, but I remember crying because I could never escape any of the entrapments he set up. Grandma would come to rescue me right away, which meant punishment for him. He was Grandma's baby boy, and my mother was Grandma's baby girl.

I never dreaded going back home that I can remember, but I do remember the punishments my siblings and I had to endure. I cannot imagine what we could have done wrong, but I remember that we would be lined up in the living room and had to stand in a sort of at-ease position, looking up at the ceiling. The punishments seemed to me to have gone on for hours and would hurt like hell after a while. My poor little brothers would cry, fall to the floor, and get spanked, only to have to do it all over again.

As a kid, watching this at the time seemed like torture. I am sure I did not know what torture was, but it was unexplainable, and I wished someone would walk in and stop my mother's boyfriend.

My mother worked at the hospital, and I take it that is where she was when she wasn't home. I take it her boyfriend would care for us in her absence, and until recent years, I did not understand that this is what we sometimes do as women. We put our trust in the man we date or fall in love with and assume that the way he presents himself as feeling for us, he feels for our children. I must believe that my mother did not know the other side of him or what he was doing to her children.

When I was in school, I would anxiously wait for the time to come for me to go to school. There was a song that went "toot-toot hey beep-beep, hey mister you got a dime" by Donna Summer from the song, Bad Girl. Every time that song would play in the morning, I honestly thought that was my cousins calling from across the hall so we could go to school.

The "Hey, Mister" portion of the song sounded like "Hey, Risa," which was my nickname, and I would run out of my room and say they were ready, and once I walked out the door, I would realize they were not calling me after all. It felt good to get out of the house, so I never went back to tell them that it was not my cousins.

As I stated, my aunt and cousins lived across the hall, and they were my playmates often. They were older than I was and always appeared to be having more fun than I was.

My older cousins and I would always walk to school together in the mornings. I always seemed to be the focus of their attention when they wanted to play practical jokes. I would cry often, and eventually got used to the practical jokes. We would stop by the store before or after school to buy candy.

I always envied them as older cousins because they would buy things I couldn't. One day, I was determined to do what my older cousins did as they brought their candy. So, I left the school grounds and did not wait for them. I think I was around the age of seven or eight. I walked to the store and bought a piece of "Gatorade" gum.

Uh, this was the moment I had dreamed of. I did it! Now, I would go home and be proud that I did a big girl move. As I was attempting to cross on my own, I was hit by a car.

The details I remember are vague, but I remember my mother arriving on the scene and riding in the ambulance with me. All I could think about was this: I'm going to get it! I was wrong; she showed compassion by telling me I shouldn't have done that. I remember I was the center of her attention for a while, and then that wore off.

I have vague details about my mother and very little memory, as she died when I was young. I believe I was around 8 or 9 years old, somewhere in that range. I was at home in our bedroom and remember hearing voices one night, saying she was killed while crossing the street.

Reflecting on that moment, I realize how important it is to be careful of the conversations around children, even when we think they are not listening. Even with my children, I have taken for granted how much they hear, see, and know. No one knew how much I had heard about the accident, or that I realized that my mother was never coming back home, nor did anyone discuss this moment with me.

From what I heard, my mother was out with my other aunts one night when the accident happened. I recall hearing cries of distress and chaos, and I joined in the commotion. This incident was my second traumatic experience, my first being the fire.

God is Enough

"The Lord is nigh unto them that are of a broken heart; and saveth such as be of a contrite spirit." –
Psalm 34:18 (KJV)

Even before I understood what was happening to me, God was there. I was too young to form the words, but He was there. Reflecting on this time in my life, I can appreciate that I survived.

Have you ever felt like your pain began before you had a chance to find your voice? Pause and remember: God was near then, and He's near now. Take a moment to reflect on where He kept you, even in what you couldn't control.

Chapter 2:
Identity Crisis

Growing up, I started to notice the quiet differences between myself and the people raising me. Although my family surrounded me, something always felt slightly... off. I didn't have the language back then to name the feeling, but deep inside, I knew I was different. I was cared for, but not completely seen. As I grew older, questions began to form like whispers in my mind. Who am I? Where do I really come from? Why don't I feel fully accepted or understood? This feeling wasn't just about where I lived or who fed me — it was about a more profound longing to know where I truly belonged.

Many significant events occurred during this period, accompanied by numerous changes. My newest sibling had been born by now, and he remained with his father. My younger siblings and I went to stay with my great-aunt, who we would now know as our mother ("Mom"), after the death of my mother. I also had the chance to meet my father's side of the family, which, as far as I knew, was my first encounter with them.

I don't think I was ten yet at this time in my life, but I know that I had experienced a lot in my short lifespan. I knew we were no longer being punished like we had been, which was a great relief. I spent more time outside with my cousins, who began to show a different side of what used to be the center of pranks. I ran, laughed, played, and experienced my first prank from a non-family member. It was a little boy named Maurice who thought it was funny to pull my pants down while I was trying to swing on the monkey bars. Kids will always be kids—that's all I can say about that.

The transition with my siblings and me happened pretty quickly, and we moved from where Mom once lived to our new dwelling place with my great-aunt, "Mom." I don't remember feeling sad during this time—and that's not to say I wasn't—but I believe that an intervention during this period was needed.

When tragedy strikes in the life of children, and they're removed from their known surroundings, I think they need therapy, at some level. There should be an intervention for a short while to ensure the children can adjust and function appropriately.

When we moved into our new home, we had much more space. We had my great uncle, who would become our new "Father," and my cousin, who would become our new "Brother."

It came to be that seven of us lived in one apartment that was eventually divided into two apartments. I don't know how that happened, but it worked. We had more room than we ever could have remembered. Life, as I knew it, was good. I didn't have to wash dishes; we ate at the table like a family, which was something I was not used to.

As stated, my cousin became my new "Brother" and was just a month younger than me. He and I would always get into something. I remember he had toys and games my siblings and I didn't have when we moved in, but not long after we moved in, his toys and games became "ours" and not just his. I'm sure this was difficult for him—being the only child for a while and now having to share with four others—but this was how it was.

I learned to iron to take the "cat faces" out of "Mom's" work shirts and even wear some of her socks. I remember telling her that her socks were my socks, and she had to explain that they were hers—then she brought me some of my own.

When I was young, I don't know how she managed to do it with five kids and work, but she did. Between all the Christmas holidays, birthdays, Easter Sundays, and school days, we always had something. It wasn't until I became an adult that I understood all she went through to ensure we had something.

As I began to get older, "Brother" and I would be sent to the store, and in my mind, I was once again on the road to being the big girl I felt I was. "Mom" would give us money to buy enough candy for all five of us, and I believe the candy was about three for a penny or something like that. We would watch her separate the candy into five rows and get a row of at least five pieces.

"Father" worked at some facility that either manufactured or shipped costume jewelry. I recall receiving small chains and necklaces from him frequently.

While they worked, we had another aunt who babysat us and several of my cousins. She lived in the same building, but downstairs from us.

This normal childhood was finally introduced to me. Not that we didn't get beatings or weren't punished for wrongdoing—because we were—but there was fun and laughter along with it. We had friends in the building and on the block, and it seemed like we were just carefree and able to be kids in those days.

In the street, we played tops, a street game, using chalk or crayons to create boxes. We had roller skates—and oh my gosh, when I think about those roller skates made like shoes, you'd push the button so the wheels would come out! Those were the days. We played Double Dutch almost every day and scrambled to find a spot in the shade where we could escape the sun.

We lived right next door to the fire department, and sometimes, they would turn on the hydrant in the summer, and we would get wet. I don't remember having block parties back then, but it sure felt like one on some nights when the sun went down, because everyone and their mother would be outside.

We had an older white man on the block named "Bobby." I think Bobby was everyone's friend, and I don't remember if he had any kids, but I think we all were his kids in his way.

We would wait for Bobby to come home from work, which was around 5 pm, and run to his window to call him. He knew what the call was for and would open the window, telling us to give him a minute. We would stand there and wait, and Bobby would come back with a little plastic bag filled with quarters for each of us. I don't know if we ever thanked him for the money, but I do know we rushed to the store as fast as possible to get our goodies. Candy, cookies, icies, and chips were on our menu. There was straight silence for a minute while we indulged in what we had.

I loved vanilla and chocolate ice cream, a hard candy called 'Now and Laters,' and even pickled pig feet in the jar. We would eat our junk food and go back to playing.

During that time, the shoes, jellies, were out, and we all had different colored jelly shoes and jackets. On hot days, that stuff was hot, and on cool days, it was cool—but no matter what day you had those jelly shoes on, you could believe your feet were dirty with the sequence or design of those shoes.

My maternal grandmother would still come around at least once a week and have Bible study with me. I used to dread those days. It would only be for about an hour, but I felt like I was the only kid being pulled from playing to go and study The Bible. I had my Bible and a yellow book called *My Book of Bible Stories*, which we studied. I remember she and another lady would come, but sometimes Grandma would visit alone.

Every week after Bible study, she would have me study and memorize a few books of The Bible, and she would test my knowledge when she returned. I eventually learned all of them—and not by choice. Little did I know, she taught me what I now need in my adult life and how to use it daily.

Grandma would jump rope with us sometimes after Bible study or even chat for a minute outside. She had a smile that always lit my heart. Grandma could have had the worst days, but you would never have known it because she would smile and say, "I am okay and doing well."

We all smile to hide some of our pain.

As time went by, I began to experience what it felt like to be molested. I was probably nine or ten at this time, but I'm not sure, as I could have been a little older. I never let "Mom" know, and I am not sure why. Perhaps because she was going through her domestic issues with "Father" at the time. He always told me to shower, and I used to dread it because I knew what would happen. He would teach me how to wash myself, and then his fingers would end up between my legs. He said this was how it was supposed to be, and I dared not challenge him. Taking a shower for me was a stressful moment. Can you even imagine a grown man taking advantage of a young girl? He didn't have any remorse.

"Mom" worked hard, cooking, cleaning, and caring for five busy children daily. I don't think she ever had a break from all of us at once. I didn't know it then, but she was happily married with one child when she took us in, and this must have been rough on her, having to care for the four of us.

I would also get visits from my father's mother on the weekends. She began to pick me up, take me shopping, and then take me to her home. There was one visit that started a spiral of extra-special visits.

My paternal grandmother picked me up and took me home to meet my father, who was waiting at her house. He was asleep on the floor, wrapped in a quilt. I remember walking into this dark room with the lights off, Grandma holding my hand. She tapped him, and he awoke with a smile on his face.

"Hey, baby girl," he said.

I didn't know then that he was my biological father, but I soon found out. I wasn't a baby, but I was his baby, and he held me as if he had just seen me for the first time. The hugs and attention felt good, and I enjoyed every moment of it.

We went through pictures, went to the store and back, and laughed and played until it was time for me to go home. My paternal grandmother was faithful in coming to get me, and our routine never changed. She took me to the store to eat—I think this was when McCrory's had a little eatery. We would eat, shop, and then go home.

While Grandma was either cleaning or cooking, Dad would take me outside to play. We played in the snow, in the sun, or in the yard. These visits went on for some time.

"Mom" and the rest of the family moved to a new house. This house was huge and had two stories and an attic. My aunt and cousins, who lived in the apartment building with us, moved to the first floor of the new house. My sister and I shared a room, while my brothers shared another.

We were a little older now and no longer required a sitter. I was around 12 years old.

Bobby continued to be known for quarters. He gave them to us every other Saturday, along with pizza and drinks. He even began taking us on trips to the World Trade Center. We met new friends and still had a great time. As the oldest, it was my responsibility to watch the younger ones and ensure the house remained clean. We were not allowed outside until "Mom" was home from work, but we snuck out anyway. We would all be in different places, but we were expected to be back home by the time she arrived.

During this time, more of the dysfunction in my life began. "Father" had become more comfortable with molesting me. He would wake me up in the middle of the night, and he would take off my panties. I would be asleep on the top bunk bed, and he would maneuver his way by reaching over the rail. Sometimes, I remember crying because I was terrified and did not want him touching me. He would coach me by saying, "Shhhhhh. Mom is asleep, and I don't want to wake her." He would teach me how to hide my panties. He said, "No, one should see your panties." I would lie there on the floor with my legs open while he moved his penis up and down on my little vaginal area. What satisfaction could he have been getting from this?

"Father" had his biological son, my "brother," in the house, and, as I said, we were born a month apart. "Father" did not pull any punches with him. "Brother" used to steal things, and we were beaten for it. He would lie, say he didn't, and sometimes get caught. Eventually, his beatings caused him to want to beat us, and the drama became worse.

"Brother" and I were the oldest two in the house, but my siblings and I were all afraid of him for some reason. He would say jump, and we would do it. One thing about "Mom" is that if one did something, we all might as well have done it because we were all getting beaten for it.

In my mind and heart, this was unfair because I believed by now that she had to know it was not all of us, but it was "Brother." I mean, this boy stole, and stole, and stole, and we would cry out, 'We did not do it,' and get beaten. Even our cousins who lived downstairs would sometimes get beaten for the same reasons because we were all together. The family motto was that everyone was punished if one did something wrong.

One night, when I was being molested, something happened. I don't know if it was her intuition or me crying, but "Mom" walked in on his act. I was in bed with no panties on, my legs open, and crying, and he was standing there. Thankfully, this encounter marked the end of his disgusting acts and the end of my having to live with a child molester. Needless to say, this would not be the end of the darkness I was living with. Although I was a child, I wondered, "What happens now?"

God is Enough

"Before I formed thee in the belly I knew thee; and before thou camest forth out of the womb I sanctified thee..." – Jeremiah 1:5 (KJV)

As I grew older, I spent years trying to figure out who I was — piecing my identity together through rejection, silence, and unanswered questions. But God knew me before any of it. Before the labels, the trauma, and before the search for a sense of belonging. I wasn't a mistake or a burden — I was *chosen* and *set apart* by a God who already had a purpose for my life, even when "Father" knew me, God still knew me best. I was already known on a level that only God knew He could heal.

Are you still searching for identity in the echoes of what others said or did, or didn't say and didn't do? Pause and ask yourself: *What does it mean to be known by God before anyone else had a chance to define me?* Let that truth silence every lie that tries to tell you otherwise.

Chapter 3:
Unchosen But Not Unclaimed

Everything I thought I knew about love, safety, and family began to unravel like a loose thread. I couldn't explain how or when the shift happened, but I could feel it deep in my spirit. The promises, the dreams, and the small hopes I had held onto started slipping through my fingers. I was losing control, and even worse, I was losing myself. This chapter marks the part of my story where survival turned into daily endurance, and silence became my shield.

I don't know what "Mom" said to "Father," but I know they separated after he was caught. I do remember her telling me to keep 'this' information between us. I didn't realize it then—and probably wouldn't have because I was a kid myself—but she was hurt. Hell, I was hurt, too.

As a child, I wondered questions like, "How did this happen? Did she know how long this was going on? Was it my fault? Was I going to be in trouble?" These questions went through my mind as I was confused and scared.

As a child, I knew I did things that often got me into trouble, and when it happened, I wasn't surprised. However, this situation wasn't of my own making.

After things quieted down at home, I remember lying awake at night, wrapped tightly in a blanket or sheet, with thoughts of him still coming into my room. Even as I share this truth from my adulthood now, I wonder how he could attempt oral sex on a minor?

Thinking back to my childhood, I couldn't explain what I felt, nor did I have anyone to explain it to.

Somehow, life went on, and there were no discussions. We continued to be a family without him, and he never returned.

I think this is the point at which I began to form uncertainty about myself and to seek out something, without knowing what it was.

I was a preteen (around ages 12-13) and started liking the little boy, Ray, across the street from us. I would play with the other girls, but I was more interested in playing with him.

Ray was cute to me at the time and would arrange with my "Brother" to have me come over to his house at a particular time. Since my siblings and I were all scared of my "Brother" and knew he could get us in trouble, getting me to do what he wanted was not hard at all. Besides, I liked Ray and didn't mind spending time with him—even if it was a gain for my "brother."

If he ever decided he wanted to get me in trouble, my "Brother" had this boyfriend of mine over my head. It was like his trump card.

My "Brother" was special to his mom, and I always felt he had special treatment. Once his father was forced to move out, he started sleeping in his mother's bed with her while we all slept in our beds. I began to rebel. I thought, "Why was he the only one who had the opportunity to sleep with 'Mom?'" I thought this because, after all, she was our "Mom," too, right?

I secretly envied in my little heart that my "Brother" got to sleep with "Mom." But it was during some family time moments that we had that allowed me to see what went on in the bedroom. As I got older, I put the pieces together. During family time, we would sit in the living room as kids, playing games, eating junk food, or whatever. In between the jokes and conversation with us, I recall them having conversations or making jokes about how the two of them slept in different positions. For instance, he would say that he was able to sleep in the 'chair,' which meant that she slept on her side with her legs folded, somewhat in a chair position with her knees bent, and he slept in front of her with his rear end resting on her knees. As a child, it sounded cool, and I imagined her arms wrapped around him. She would also chime in and sometimes jokingly tell him that he would no longer sleep in that position. I don't remember how old she was, but I do remember he was around the age of 12 or 13. This 'sleeping together' went on for a good while.

Reflecting on my life up to that point, I accepted a profound truth: whether it is through foster care, extended family, or close friends, I discovered that people do not always genuinely love someone else's children as their own. I think they can love someone else's child, but there is a special bond between parent and child that cannot be duplicated—unless you raise that child from infancy. This thought became my truth.

As time passed, I began to develop both physically and mentally, and this growth started to show. I began to build my own identity and want my own things. It started to sink in that I was adopted, and this life is what it was because my mother was gone. I began to see other relationships with parents and children, which I envied. It was a hidden jealousy, pain, and desire within my heart.

I was no longer receiving many visits from my paternal or maternal grandmothers, and I didn't know why—this was just how it was. I had my friends, and we would do things regularly. They were hanging out, and I wanted to do the same. We had family functions and parties, and on the inside, I was broken. No one knew it; honestly, I did not know it at the time, either.

I knew I had endured and done some things, but I felt more like I was in a Twilight Zone. I was no longer the happy kid that I once was.

I recall writing a letter to my maternal grandmother, telling her about what had happened. I recall her talking to me, although I don't remember the exact details of the conversation. Shortly after, I recall staying with my paternal grandparents. I was around the age of 13 or 14. Dad was not there as often, but when he was, he made it worthwhile. I also found out I had a little brother with my father and his new wife.

I was able to confide in my dad, so I told him what happened and the instances where I was molested. He was furious. As I recall, he told me I would never be in that situation again. I believed him because he was my dad and my protector.

Not long after I moved in with my paternal grandparents, my dad went down South with his new wife. He was arrested for a crime he didn't commit and was only found not guilty after his death. While he was gone, I stayed with my grandmother and grandfather. I felt lost all over again.

Dad had promised to change my name to a Muslim name and said I'd come live with him once they got settled. But time passed, and he never came back. I missed him terribly. My protector—the one who listened, loved me, and called me his "little girl"—was gone.

As my brother and I were officially living with my paternal grandparents, my other siblings lived with "Mom." I hated that we were separated, but I guess it was what was best for those who cared for us.

By this time, I felt like Grandma couldn't understand me. She worked long hours and came home exhausted, still trying to care for my brother and me. She asked for help with chores, but I didn't want to do anything—not babysit, not clean. I just wanted to escape the chaos I had come from.

Grandpa was there, always reading his Bible. But we didn't talk. I couldn't go to him. I felt invisible. He hadn't always been like that. I remembered when he'd be gone all day and come home drunk.

Life was different now than when Grandma used to take me out on the weekends. It felt like she became responsible for me since my dad was not there. It felt like she needed to establish some rules to maintain order around the house. I was older and had chores, schoolwork, homework, and church. We attended church almost every day. Every time I turned around, we had some event in church. We had prayer services, choir practices, meetings, Sunday school, afternoon services, and even plays for the holidays. We had breakfast, lunch, and dinner in church on Sundays.

I couldn't go outside until Grandma came home from work. She worked at a factory all day and came home. Her legs would be tired and achy, but she would keep on going. She had me, my brother, and sometimes my little cousins to care for. I would have to cook and clean by the time Grandma got home from work, or I would be punished. I didn't want to cook, clean, or babysit. I wanted to have fun and do 'me!'

I didn't really get beatings, but I was punished a lot. I refused to do what I was asked to do, and I knew in my early teens that I was grown. When Grandma was at work, I would blast my music and party. Although I was not supposed to, I would have company. I knew how to have everything straightened up by the time Grandma came in from work. I was very outspoken and swore I knew what I was doing.

Here is when I had my first actual boyfriend, as I knew it. I would sneak out when Grandma went to work and spend time with him. We went to the same school and waited for each other after school. He was slow compared to me—after all, I had experience in this area, and I wanted to hold hands and kiss, but he wouldn't dare. He had the fear that his mother would think this was not right. He also had the fear and respect for my grandmother that I didn't have—to know we should not be doing this.

I would frequently be mad at him for not giving in to me. We broke up, and we both moved on to high school. I started high school and immediately met some new friends in addition to those from elementary school. I started participating in school activities just to get out of the house. That did not last long, because eventually, I was not allowed to participate in any school festivities after I was caught hanging out.

I had another boyfriend and then another one. But the next one, I thought this one was going to be my future. Willie was a Junior, and I was a Freshman in high school. He was different than the 'little' boys I had been seeing. He was a man. He was muscular, built, and dark-skinned. He reminded me of my father. His family and I went to the same church and sang in the same choir. We were all in church for the same long hours, which was one good reason for me to continue attending church and all the services.

My grandmother noticed us getting close and tried to put an end to it. I gave her a run for her money. My dad, who was still alive when I was dating this guy, would call from prison. I would tell him how much I loved this man. My dad would never ask me to leave him; he would encourage anything that made his little girl happy. That was my dad, good, bad, or indifferent, and I love him for that.

I think I was about 14 and head over heels for this man. He would meet me at school and walk me home. Although a church boy, he had a well-known reputation for fighting, so no one would bother him—or me. We dated for a long time, and I got pregnant. We were both ecstatic. My grandmother was blowing steam for a long time. I now realize she meant well and had my best interests in mind, but I couldn't see it at the time.

To me, Grandma was too strict, and I could not do anything outside of going to church. I just wanted to have fun like everyone else and enjoy my boyfriend! All I knew was that I had the man I loved; he had me, and we were having a baby. His parents seemed happy for us and wanted us to get married. Again, this was right up my alley. We were making plans, he bought a ring, his mother was fixing dinners and inviting me, and I was living at home on cloud nine with an attitude that said, 'I am grown and about to do things my way.'

At that time, this seemed to both sides of the family like the right thing to do since we were Christians and did not want to live outside of God's will. However, I ended up having a miscarriage in my grandmother's living room. I didn't know at the time that it was a miscarriage, but it was excruciating pain. I was balled up on the floor, screaming for Jesus.

I never really asked my grandmother for anything, but I was begging for her help that night. Usually, when we were ill or seemed to be getting sick, she would give us a teaspoon of castor oil or an old medicine called *666*, and this was not one of those moments when any of those medications would have helped.

I ended up in the hospital, had a miscarriage, and thought I was going to lose my mind. How did this happen? Things I thought were going so well— and from here, my world as I knew it again began to crash.

Willie came to see me in the hospital, carrying a blue binder. Blue is my favorite color, and he knew it. I'm not sure what he had in mind with the binder, but he brought it to me anyway. He still seemed to be excited and was rubbing my stomach. He had no idea about the miscarriage. I told him quickly, and he burst into tears. He was silent for a long while. I didn't know what he was thinking. But in my mind, I felt that we could try again and be happy again.

He had other plans in mind. He was mad at my grandmother. He just knew she was behind me having a miscarriage—and I thought so, too. I thought she prayed for this. When I saw my grandmother, I felt she was happy that this was happening to me. I resented her for this.

After a while, Willie began to distance himself. He stopped coming around, started selling drugs, and lived what I thought was 'the life.' When he came around, he was dressed nicely, with shining jewelry and gold teeth. Beepers were out at the time, and he had one.

Finally, one day, he told me that he could not continue seeing me because my grandmother would not allow it to happen. He would not be restricted to staying at home and seeing me during the day. He was attending parties, and I was not allowed to go. His actions hurt me and, at the same time, made me angry. I had mixed feelings, but I was determined to see my man.

I began to make up lies about going to choir practice in the evening just to be able to see him. I ran away from home a few times just to spend the night with him. I would go to the clubs and hangouts where he would be, and he would be in the presence of other girls. I didn't care because he was my man, no matter how anyone saw it. I wanted him, and I would do anything—and I mean anything—to get him back.

He didn't want me back, and this hurt. He saw me as a 'good' girl, not a street girl. "This is not you," he would say. He would also say, "Go back home to your grandmother and go to church." He began to joke about me in front of his friends, which also hurt me. I would show him that I was more than a church girl—I could hang out too—but I had to figure out how.

As I continued to pursue him, I remember a time when the weather began to turn cold on the streets, and I had no shelter. All my friends were in for the night, and I was alone, walking the streets and sleeping in hallways. This life was not the life I wanted to live.

Looking back, I now see how broken pieces began to accumulate without being addressed. The more I tried to hold it together, the more it fell apart around me. I didn't have the words then, but I was crying out for help in the only ways I knew how. That season reminded me that God sees even the silent battles, and while I didn't realize it at the time, He was already preparing my path forward—even in the midst of the wreckage.

God is Enough

"When my father and my mother forsake me, then The Lord will take me up." – Psalm 27:10 (KJV)

I didn't ask to be moved from home to home or to live under the weight of uncertainty and survival. But even in instability, God remained steady. Even when it felt like no one chose me, He had already claimed me as His own. I wasn't just a child of the system — I was still a child of God. And where man failed me, God never left my side.

Have you ever felt abandoned by the very people who were supposed to protect you? Let this truth anchor you: *When others let go, God takes hold.* His love isn't temporary. It's eternal, and it's already holding you.

Chapter 4:
Trapped in the Cycle

When your soul is suffocating, escape becomes more than an option—it becomes your only hope. I didn't always know how to describe what I was running from, but I felt the desperation in my chest with every breath. I thought if I could just get away—physically, emotionally, spiritually, I could start over. But even as I tried to leave behind what was hurting me, I realized some wounds don't stay in one place. They follow you, live inside you, and wait to be healed.

I couldn't go back to my grandmother's house because I had made a fool of myself, and she would never let me go out the way I wanted—at least, this is what I told myself. So, I went from one friend's house to another and then to one of my aunt's houses. My aunt let me sleep on her sofa.

By this time, I was 15 years old and had dropped out of high school. I was legally an emancipated minor. I needed no one's permission. I was running wild.

Every so often, I would think about the fact that no one was looking for me, which also made me feel that no one cared if I was dead or alive. I suppose *they* figured if I were grown, then I should be treated as such. I summed that up to mean I had no parents here. And if I did, my father, who hadn't passed away at this time, I thought that he would have been looking for me. Then, perhaps I wouldn't have even been in the situation, because he wouldn't have allowed it.

I chased after Willie until I had had enough pain from seeing him with other women and him brushing me off. I think his last encounter with me was at his grandmother's house late one night. I went there to see him after he called me. I thought I was spending the night with him—this night, I was excited, thinking we would finally be back together.

We ate, had sex, and then he told me I had to leave. I don't mean asking me to leave—I mean literally putting me out. Grabbing my things, telling me I had to go. I felt dirty and disgusted. How could he have loved me at one time, cared so much about protecting me, and yet put me out of his house?

Who was this person? What happened to the man I was in love with? I felt used. I refused to leave, and he grabbed me as if he could have killed me if I didn't go. He pushed me out the door and threw my stuff outside, too. I was so hurt and angry that I walked the avenue crying. It had to be about 2 a.m. or later.

I recall being taken to the precinct and questioned about what had happened. The officers wanted to know if I was raped, and I told them yes. I told them he raped me and threw me out. Although this was not true, I did not care at the time; I just wanted him to hurt the way I hurt. They called my grandmother and took me to the hospital. I don't think charges were pressed against him because my story came out about how we were in a relationship, and I couldn't get past it.

I ended up in the hospital a few other times for bad urinary tract infections and other things because I was not taking care of myself.

I was still around the age of 15, living from house to house or hallway to roof, wherever I could lay my head.

One day, one of my older male cousins saw me outside at the crack of dawn, and he slapped the living daylights out of me. He told me to take my butt home, but where was home? He had no idea I was living on the street.

I was two blocks from my "Mother's" house, so I went there. She was at work, and I was knocked out on her sofa when she came home. She never mentioned it, but I think she knew I was staying on the streets. My clothes were dirty, and I can only imagine what my hair looked like. On the first day, I was extremely hungry. I ate like a hound dog after she cooked.

I don't recall the details, but I ended up staying home again. I knew I had to follow "Mom's" rules. Nevertheless, I thought I was grown and was determined to do what I wanted to do.

Returning to "Mom's" house, I still had the same friends who would see me. We would hang out and get drunk. I would miss curfew and be grounded, which didn't stop my friends from coming around. We would hang out in my hallway until I was off punishment. When I was off punishment, I was back at it again.

We walked all over Jersey City. You name the town—we were there. My friends' moms all thought I was the fastest one. Little did they know, birds of a feather flock together, if you get my drift?

My friends' mothers swore up and down I was going to get pregnant and have children and not be able to hang out, which did happen, but not until years later. Their daughters' children are older than mine, which means I was the last out of the bunch to get pregnant.

I had a lot of issues going on in my life, and was searching for happiness. I wasn't happy at home, I wasn't satisfied on the street—I just was not pleased. I didn't know I had been broken and not repaired. In fact, I don't think anyone took the time to see that. I believe everyone saw what they wanted to see.

I had encounters with other family members, and I'm sure they were told I was misbehaving. But no one took the time to find out what was happening in my life and why. No one sought counseling, a group home, or anything that could have possibly drawn me back in. I always held in the back of my mind that I was on my own and needed to take care of myself. I saw myself as a bad kid and not wanted by anyone.

I needed counseling, but I was the one who was giving counseling sessions to my younger siblings. Yet, today, when I look back at those days, I had some issues, but professional counseling was not a big thing in families, especially Black families. Everything was a secret, and no one talked openly about anything in the family.

By now, my older adopted brother, "Brother," had picked up some of his father's traits, and it seemed the patterns were starting to repeat themselves in our home again. Only now, he was a young teen like me and felt he could have his way with whomever he pleased. I was still a little scared of him, but quickly grew out of that stage.

About a year or two later, I met the man who is now my children's father. My friends and I were all hanging out and drinking at the waterfront area. I drank some MD 20/20, a strong liquor, and this made me so drunk that I was sick. I was throwing up all over the place and could not go home like that.

Kenny—his name—kept me out with him until I felt better. He kept me out until early morning after the sun came up. I knew I was in trouble. How would I explain this one? I couldn't. I was grounded again, but only for a short time.

By then, I think my "Mom" was tired of my nonsense and figured I would make my bed and lie in it.

I went out again and again, and Kenny and I began seriously seeing each other. I was a young teenager, and he told me he was 19 years old. I thought he wasn't too old for me at all. I liked the idea of being with an older guy, as he was protecting me. I liked that he was driving and knew how to have a good time. He was attentive to my little wants—buying snacks from the store when I had no money, taking me out to eat—and he would often talk about the many interesting things I liked to do, such as movies, roller skating, and dancing.

Kenny lived in New York and would travel back and forth to visit me and his friends who were nearby. We had relations frequently, and he began to become physically abusive and jealous.

The first time I experienced abuse, I saw one of my ex-boyfriends, who hugged me. I told him that I was going to see him at the club that night, and Kenny was so angry, as if I had cheated on him. He apologized and told me he was jealous. He said he didn't want to lose me, and I felt bad for him.

Additionally, other changes occurred. The friends I was with when we met—he no longer wanted me with them. The cute hairstyles and outfits I had when I met him were no longer permissible in his presence.

Kenny would slowly but surely make me do what he wanted. I would be asleep in my bed, and he would climb into my window. How he climbed up our mini roof is beyond me. I would be on punishment and not able to come out, which eventually worked for me, not seeing him, but he would find his way over there to threaten me about not seeing him.

My "Mom" knew he was my boyfriend and eventually came to like him, but she had no idea how intense my fear was. One day, he had me call and tell her I would not return home. During the call, she said, "Okay, whatever," and hung up the phone. She would drink on the weekends, and this was a weekend call, so she was drinking that night. And anyway, I couldn't dare tell her that my eye was busted and my lips were swollen from being beaten so badly.

As the abuse continued, this man would beat me if he thought I was looking at someone or even if I had been five minutes late coming from the store—anything. I was raped over and over by him because, by now, he knew that I did not want to be with him. I had to beg him to stay with me so that he wouldn't beat me for the thoughts he had of me leaving him.

As things got worse, he would sniff cocaine and want me to sniff with him, but I couldn't. I had to take a beating for that because I was too scared to put drugs in my body. I prayed and prayed for a miracle from God, and nothing happened.

I lived down the street from my paternal grandmother at the time, and several times, both she and my aunts intervened, and he would be right back with me. He would beg, plead, and tell me how much he loved and needed me. Then, once I was back in his presence alone, he would beat the crap out of me.

Around 1987, we moved to the Bronx to stay with his mother. I had no choice because he was not leaving me alone, and I had nowhere else to go. He would threaten to hurt both my grandmothers if I didn't go with him.

In December of 1988, my father died. I think this was probably the only time I could get away from Kenny, without him following me or looking for me. All those years, my dad was in prison, and now he passed away, which was a devastating moment for me. However, I found out about his passing in a challenging way.

I called my grandmother one day to see how she was doing, and she told me the funeral was arranged. "What funeral? Who died?" I asked her. She had no idea that I did not know my father had died. She apologized, but he was gone nonetheless.

I had previously experienced the loss of him when he left New Jersey and went South. He was missing from my life then, and I had to endure that, which seemed like death at the time. His physical death only meant that I would never hear his voice again and put confirmation to what I had already felt in my heart. My dad was gone for good.

We had the funeral in the South. I stayed for a few more days after the funeral and then went back to NY.

The crazy part about my father's funeral was that when I called my grandmother before knowing he had passed, I was calling my grandmother, hoping she would ask me to come back home to her place. Perhaps I should have been strong enough to tell her I wanted to return home, but I couldn't. I was embarrassed, broken, and afraid.

A few years later (around the age of 1990), I had my first son and then my daughter; by then, we were moving back and forth in NJ. In the next chapter, I'll share more about what led me to have children.

Although I was around 19 years old and I had already experienced much abuse from Kenny, I continued to be with him, and the abuse only got worse. This man used to drive around with me in the car in cold temperatures, with the windows down, and I had on only a T-shirt and maybe some sweatpants and socks.

No coat, no hat, and no gloves. He would often take my children to New York; the only way I would get them back was to ride with him.

Other times, he would take wire hangers, beat me, and kick me. I swear, at times, I felt like I would pass out and come to—and he was still beating me. At times, I could not walk or sit because of being in so much pain. You would think that would be enough for me to leave him alone, but it wasn't.

He would find and date other young girls, and I would run after him, but I still wanted him to be with me. What was wrong with me? Why couldn't I leave him alone? Or was I feeling like he was all I had at the time?

People would talk about how I deserved better and should have just left, but I couldn't. Mentally, I was trapped and did not know how to get out.

I have come to realize now, in my days, that domestic violence is serious, and it's not as easy as people say to get out. You want to, but you're afraid to let go, especially when you don't have the support that tells you or shows you that things will be okay.

Every time I thought about leaving, I thought about him finding me and hurting me, or my family. I lived with this feeling repeatedly.

Only God carried me through all those days.

No one truly understood what I was carrying, not even me. I was searching for safety in all the wrong places, hoping that the next move would finally set me free. But with every attempt to escape, I found myself more tangled in pain. Still, God kept me. Even in my confusion, He protected what was left of me. This part of my journey wasn't just about leaving—it was about learning how to face what I hadn't yet healed.

God is Enough

"Behold, what manner of love The Father hath bestowed upon us, that we should be called the sons of God..." – 1 John 3:1 (KJV)

I longed to belong—to be claimed, protected, and loved in a way that made me feel whole. I chased acceptance, tried to fit in, and hid my pain behind the mask of laughter and independence. But all along, God had already called me His. His love didn't come with conditions or shame. He gave me identity when others gave me silence. In Him, I belong — entirely, freely, and forever.

Have you been chasing love or acceptance from people who can't give you what only God can? Let today be the moment you remember: You are already loved and already seen, already called His, and that is more than enough.

Chapter 5:
Open Doors

At this time in my life, I had already carried more trauma than most adults. But pain wears many disguises—sometimes as anger, other times as fierce independence. I didn't know how to put my feelings into words, so I acted out what I couldn't process. I was starving for freedom, desperate to belong, and running from a weight I didn't know how to name. What felt like "open doors" back then were really escape hatches—small windows I crawled through, hoping they'd lead somewhere safe.

Before I had children with Kenny, I felt like a dead woman walking. I had stopped expecting joy. I had adjusted to my reality, even when it hurt.

We lived in an apartment with nothing but a discarded mattress my grandmother found on the street. No television, just a small radio and a used sofa. He refused to buy anything new or contribute to the rent. I was surviving on welfare and food stamps, and that was the only thing keeping food on our table.

His family was sickened by the domestic violence. They urged me to leave him, but they didn't know how scared I was. I lied to them constantly—about the bruises, the stitches, the truth. But deep down, they knew, and I knew they knew.

I felt trapped and ashamed. I was too proud to run back to my family and admit the truth. In my mind, this was my punishment. I had 'played' grown too soon—and now I was paying for it.

Even now, when I talk about those days, I feel it. I feel the abuse: Every hit, every forced act, every shower where I scrubbed my body, trying to erase the pain. To this day, I still struggle to watch movies with violence. I have to change the channel. It's only by God's grace that I'm alive to tell it—and this isn't even the whole story.

The year was around 1987 or 1988, and we were living in a Brooklyn brownstone that belonged to one of his friends. We had no heat, just electricity and cold water. We boiled water for everything—bathing, warmth, and food. That's where I learned real survival. We steamed the room to keep warm. We washed our outfits every night because we had only one or two changes of clothes. I had just two pairs of panties, and he taught me how to wash them.

We cooked food on a hot plate. No pork—just lamb chops and vegetarian beans, over and over. We shopped for food together, and I learned how to make something out of nothing.

Some people might say I brought this on myself. In some ways, maybe I did. If I had stayed a child—if I had been guided, protected, or even interrupted earlier—I might have made different choices. But I didn't have that kind of intervention. I didn't know what I didn't know.

So, where does the blame really go? As a teenager, yes—I had a mouth. I had an attitude. But as a mother now, I believe more could have been done to reach me. I needed someone to chase after me the way I now chase after my children.

I vowed that my kids would never go a day without hearing from me. Even when they made choices I didn't like, I showed up. I asked questions. I checked in. I didn't leave them to "learn the hard way." I couldn't imagine them learning the way I did.

At that point in my life, I believed I was beyond repair. I thought everyone had given up on me, and honestly, I had given up on myself, too.

Around the time of my son's birth, I moved into a one-bedroom apartment, which was conveniently close to my family. When I came home with the baby, everyone came to support me. I had gifts galore, and the love poured in from my cousins and aunts who had not seen me in years. I even ended up in the same building as my best friend, whom I had not seen in years, and we were on the same floor. We talked for hours about where I had been and what was happening. We shared stories of our past and reminisced about the fun we had back then. The fellowship and joy lasted for a few days, with several hours of each day dedicated to them.

My abuser, Kenny, was gone for a couple of days, which did not bother me at all. He eventually came to my house and scooped up both me and the baby after being there for 24 hours. He took us to New York to live with him and his mother.

His mother was super kind to me. She took me under her wing as if I were her daughter. She taught me how to cook, clean, care for my son, and even tend to my wounds. When she would go to work sometimes, the fighting would start, and the torture.

I became pregnant with my daughter not even six weeks later. My children are 10 months apart today, and my daughter was born at close to 7.5 months. She was a healthy weight and was allowed to come home from the hospital when I did.

After the birth of my daughter, we moved back to NJ from NY and rented a studio. The studio was not big, but it was big enough for us since the children were small.

I was not receiving any services except WIC, which provided tremendous help at the time. I depended solely upon him to care for us, and he did, on his terms. I didn't want my children to suffer, and I had a desire to make sure they did not.

I no longer cared about my life, but I wanted my children to be safe and felt determined to get them to safety. I didn't know how I was going to do it, but I had enough determination to get it done.

Some time after we moved to NJ, we got evicted, and that day it was pouring rain outside. I think it was around 1991. I was waiting for Kenny to return and pick us up—and he didn't. This moment was right up my alley because I considered this the ideal time to escape him.

God is Enough

"There hath no temptation taken you but such as is common to man: but God is faithful, who will not suffer you to be tempted above that ye are able..." –
1 Corinthians 10:13 (KJV)

I tried to find freedom in all the wrong places. I was searching for a door that led to peace. I looked for an escape route that would set me free. But all I found were more reasons to hurt. Even then, God didn't walk away. His faithfulness was the open door I didn't know I needed. The eviction from the apartment was God's escape, even though I was left with two children.

In every consequence and every cry for help, He was still my escape. He didn't give up on me—even when I gave up on myself.

Have you been walking through doors that only lead to more pain? Have you ever tried to escape a painful situation, only to feel more trapped? Let this be your reminder: Even in your darkest moments, God remains faithful. The way out may not be what you expected, but His way is always enough.

Chapter 6:
The Great Escape

There comes a point in survival where silence no longer works. I had swallowed so many truths, buried so many violations, that my body began to ache with secrets. What I needed was an escape, not just from a place, but from the version of myself that pain had shaped. I didn't have a plan, only the will to be free. And sometimes, that's all you have. What unfolded next would test every bit of strength I didn't know I had.

After the eviction, I had no clothes to pack. So at the age of 20, with my two young children, I took what little I had, packed up their stroller, and walked to the train station. My only plan was to get back to New York. My abuser was stationed in New Jersey, and I had learned of a homeless shelter near my "Mom's" home during a previous stay with his mother. I held onto that information, hoping one day I would be brave enough to leave.

With each step toward the train station, I prayed I wouldn't run into him. I didn't have a dime, but I jumped on the train anyway—with my babies—to the city.

At the New York Emergency Assistance Unit, they helped me find a shelter. He had no idea I was back in the city—and this time, I wasn't going to tell him.

The intake process took hours. I was exhausted, the kids were hungry and crying, and I had nothing—no milk, no food. I just kept telling them we would be okay, begging them not to give up on me. I feared they would starve before we got help. But eventually, we were helped.

After intake, we received sandwiches and juice. They handed out bottled milk and baby food, cookies, and snacks. That was the best meal I'd had in days. I started stashing extras—baby bottles, diapers—until security let me know they were giving me extra to take with me. I was so relieved.

We bounced around a few two-day hotels before finally being placed in long-term housing. This shelter had educational services and daycare. I could apply for public assistance and be added to the housing waitlist. For the first time in a long while, I felt a sense of hope.

I finally felt like I was safe—I wouldn't run into him in Queens, New York. But as fate would have it, I ran into his brother-in-law. He was seeing someone at the same hotel where I was placed. I didn't even have to say anything. Deep down, I knew he would tell him where I was.

Sure enough, I was found.

I was sitting outside one day when my worst nightmare pulled up in a car. Right there, in front of everyone, he grabbed me and started hitting me. He had no regard for our children or the people watching. The police were called, and this time, they arrested him. But unlike before, he stayed in jail for years. The state proceeded with prosecution, whether I picked them up or not.

Finally, I was free again. But freedom came at a price. I had stitches going up my wrist, a sling for my arm, and a missing tooth. I was too young for this much pain—but at least, for now, it was over.

I cried myself to sleep many nights. I couldn't focus on my children the way I needed to. I wanted to take a break, but there was no such thing as a break. I wanted to die—but who would care for my babies if I did?

My mind wouldn't stop racing. I had to manage physical wounds, mental trauma, and the weight of motherhood—all at once.

The questions haunted me: Why did this happen to me? Was this my punishment for running away? Was this how my life was going to end? There were no answers. Only time would tell.

While living in the hotel, I attended church services and met a few women who, like me, were trying to obtain Section 8 housing. They were all from New York and had family support. I didn't. They were there by choice; I was there because I had nowhere else to go.

I stayed in touch with my children's grandmother, who also lived in New York, but I couldn't visit her. I was too afraid of running into him again. That fear shaped every decision I made.

A year or two passed, and I finally had my apartment in New York. I hadn't heard from him—and didn't want to—but the fear of seeing him again never left. Even so, I couldn't let that fear stop me from rebuilding my life.

By then, I had found the courage I didn't even know I had. I was beginning to move forward—one day at a time, one decision at a time.

I met my best friend—now my sister—and our children bonded just as we did. We shopped together, cooked together, worshiped together, and spent nights at each other's homes. It was the kind of sisterhood I had longed for. Through her, I met the man who would eventually become my husband.

From the beginning, he adored me. He adored my children, who were around two and three years old at the time. We connected like we had known each other our whole lives. He worked the night shift, and after work, we'd talk for hours until eventually, he started spending the night—and then never really left.

We had deep conversations about everything, including my childhood and the abuse I had endured. He had a bachelor's degree in psychology, so he naturally wanted to understand. He asked the hard questions, "Where was your family in all of this?" "Did anyone report you missing or call the police?" The truth was—I wondered the same.

He was against abuse in every form. He despised the man who hurt me. Moreover, he committed to protecting me. He helped me enroll in school, earn my GED, pursue an associate's degree, and even paid for me to become a home health aide and CNA. Eventually, we got married, and he adopted my children.

He promised me no one would ever hurt me again. For the first time since my father's presence in my early childhood, I felt that same love, protection, and assurance. I felt seen. But I didn't realize then, and neither did he—I was still broken.

I had clothes and jewelry like never before—and so did my children. He liked me to dress sexy, but I couldn't. I had been conditioned to hide. Every time I tried to dress up, my body remembered the beatings I had endured. I was still trying to unlearn the art of survival. But I knew how to cook, clean, and care for my children. Everything Grandma once asked me to do, I now do with confidence. The very tasks I used to resist became my strength. I cooked great meals and made our house feel like home. When I moved out of the shelter, I was given furniture vouchers, which I used to transform that apartment into a peaceful space for my children.

Still, there were pieces of me that hadn't healed. After disagreements with my husband, I would want to make up through sex—because that's what I had known. That was what I had been taught love looked like. He didn't understand it. He'd tell me, "We're married. I'm not leaving you after one argument." It took time for me to believe that love didn't have to hurt.

At first, I thought I had entered a marriage made in paradise. However, even that dream would be put to the test.

Somehow, Kenny found my number. I think it was published, and one of his children's mothers gave it to him. One day, he called me from a halfway house.

When I heard his voice, my entire body froze. It felt like a horror film—except this was my life. My husband was home, and when he saw me panic, he took the phone and told Kenny never to call again. He said, "If you ever come near my wife again, I will hurt you."

Kenny ranted, claiming I liked everything he did to me. He said I wanted the beatings. He was sick. Hearing his voice again confirmed that moving was the only option. If he had the number, he could find the address. I knew my husband would protect me, but what about when he wasn't there? I couldn't take that chance.

My husband's family embraced me like their own. His mother and sister were always present, staying overnight with my children after school. I would go to their homes to see my kids—they were that close. Their love became a lifeline.

With their support, I completed college, began working full-time, and purchased my first car. For the first time in a long time, I finally felt like I was living.

Then, life threw another blow. My husband got caught up in a situation and was arrested. He was only gone a few months, but that was long enough for the truth to come out. His beeper kept going off, and when I called one of the numbers back, I discovered he had a girlfriend.

At first, the woman avoided me. But when I finally confronted her, she admitted everything. We even met in person—she said she left something in the trunk of his car. She was a beautiful Puerto Rican woman, dressed the way he always wanted me to dress. I wondered if *that* was why he cheated.

I blamed myself. I thought I wasn't enough. I thought, maybe if I had given him what he wanted, he wouldn't have stepped out. I didn't know then that his actions were his choice, not my fault.

Still, I stayed. He was a good provider. He never hit me. He supported me and my children. He said he loved me. I wanted our family to work.

When I got pregnant with our first child together, I believed it would change things. I hoped the baby would bring us closer—that he'd be faithful. But I was wrong again. This time, I didn't catch him cheating—I *felt* it in my body.

During a routine OB/GYN visit, I was diagnosed with an STD. I was devastated. I broke down right there on the exam table. How could he do this to me? I was just two months away from giving birth. He apologized, begged for forgiveness, and I gave in again.

Two months later, I gave birth to our son. But when I went into labor and was admitted to the hospital, he was nowhere to be found. Hours passed, and then, finally, he arrived—lipstick smeared across his face.

It looked like something out of a twisted movie. He gave me some excuse about a prank while he was asleep, but I knew better. I just couldn't afford to deal with it—not while in labor, not while contractions were tearing through my body.

Eventually, he brought me roses and stayed by my side. I went home with our baby, back to our children and in-laws. For a while, life felt stable again. But less than six weeks later, it all unraveled. He cheated again, and this time, he moved out.

He told me I didn't deserve the way he treated me, that I was better off without him. That I deserved more. I should've listened. But I couldn't let him go. I loved him. We were married. He was all I had. He still provided for us, even after he left—but emotionally, I was unraveling.

I spiraled. I tried everything I could to get his attention and to hold onto what we had. I thought about suicide. I tried connecting with people who were using drugs so I could numb myself, too. I started dressing provocatively in the hope that he'd notice me again. I even reported him to his probation officer, thinking that maybe if he went to jail, I'd be the only one who would show up to visit. None of it worked.

The suicidal thoughts never turned into actions—God wouldn't let me do it. The people getting high didn't want me around, even when I offered to pay—God wouldn't let it happen. The allegations I reported didn't stick—God blocked it all.

I didn't see it then, but He was protecting me. Even in my mess, even in my madness, God had His hand on me. He wouldn't let me go.

Eventually, I was diagnosed with migraines, and instead of spiraling further, I started attending church revivals. There, I found a new kind of strength. Through every breakdown and betrayal, somehow, I kept getting back up.

I'm not saying it was easy. But I am saying—God kept me, and He never let me go.

God is Enough

> *"The name of The Lord is a strong tower: the righteous runneth into it, and is safe." – Proverbs 18:10 (KJV)*

Fear had become a daily companion. I didn't know what safety felt like anymore—until I realized that my strength wasn't in my hiding place or my hustle, it was in the name of The Lord. When I cried out, He heard me. When I ran, He covered me. He didn't just help me escape a dangerous man—He started pulling me out of a destructive mindset. The enemy wanted me stuck in fear, but God gave me power and protection.

Are you trying to escape something bigger than you? Remember: You don't have to run alone. When you run to God, you run into safety, wisdom, and peace. Let Him be your strong tower.

Chapter 7:
Rebuilding from Ruins

Starting over wasn't as glamorous as it sounds. There were no clean slates, no magical restarts—just broken pieces I had to sift through, one by one. But I was determined to try. I had made it through the fire, and now I had to figure out how to live again, not just survive. Rebuilding a new life wasn't just about changing my surroundings—it was about choosing healing every single day, even when it hurt.

My bestie and I would hang out together, pray, eat, and endure trials together. She had her issues, and I had mine.

I moved several times during the separation from my husband, thinking this was how I would get over him. Eventually, he took me to court for joint custody of the children and won. At this point, I had no other choice but to face him, when I really did not want to.

It hurt so bad to see him and not have him. He would pick up the kids on his day with his new girlfriend in the car. He would drop them off at school after his long weekend. Each week, I would wait patiently for them to come, and I would walk up to the car and start a fight with his girlfriend.

One time, he pulled off while I was holding on to the door handle of the car, trying to pull the girl out. I would never do that again. By the time I let go of the door, I had fallen and scraped up my legs, arms, and knees. I was a piece of work back then. I would do anything to get my husband back, but I learned my lesson the hard way.

We stayed separated, but we grew a different type of relationship. We became friends. He was someone I could talk to and call when I needed assistance—and vice versa. He would go through things with his girlfriend, and somehow, I became his confidant.

How this happened was beyond me, but it worked. I would give him my opinion, and he would give me his on things I was going through. We would still tell each other we had love for one another—a special kind of love, which continued despite the divorce in 2007.

One day, my abuser found out where I was living. I was living in an apartment building in the Bronx, about four floors high, and no elevators.

Somehow, he was working for the Department of Social Services and used that access to locate me. I thought I was hearing things when he called my name in the hallway. I was on the third or fourth floor, and there he was—standing right in front of my apartment door.

I froze. I thought, "Could it be? Did he really find me?"

He was yelling my name loudly, and it was embarrassing. I opened the door, and he walked in.

I know you're probably wondering why I opened the door. I don't know. Maybe it was fear. Perhaps it was shame. Maybe curiosity. But I did it.

He asked to see the kids, but something in my spirit told me this wouldn't end well. I had a 911 emergency code I used with my ex-husband, and I sent that message to him three times on my beeper. I also let him know my abuser was there.

About thirty minutes later, I found myself being thrown across the sofa, gasping for air as he choked me. The room started spinning, and then everything went dark. But he finally let go.

My son, who was about seven years old at the time, was standing nearby. My abuser asked him if he wanted to go with him, and my baby said yes. I felt like Tina Turner when Ike took her children from the bus stop in the movie, *What's Love Got to Do With It?*

I screamed and cried, begging him not to take my son, but he did. He also grabbed my house phone so that I couldn't call anyone. All I could do was pray that someone would come.

About 15 minutes later, he returned with my son, but he wouldn't leave. Instead, he lay across my bed like he belonged there.

All I could think about was the repeated sexual assaults, the bruises, and the pain. Although my ex-husband cheated—and that hurt—I would've taken that over the trauma this man caused me any day. That's how broken I was.

Why did I believe it was okay to be cheated on or abused? Why didn't I think I deserved better?

The years of trauma made it hard to think straight. I wish I had the strength back then to say, "No more." But I didn't.

At some point, I wondered why my husband didn't respond. Although we were separated, I just thought he would come through. Then I remembered. I had used our 911 code in the past to get him to come over, just to see him. I had played too many games, and maybe now, when I truly needed help, he didn't believe me.

I can't remember how much time passed, but then came a knock at the door. I didn't think—I just ran to open it. It was my ex. I hugged him so tight, thinking, *"This is the moment I've been waiting for."* I had told him before how dangerous my abuser was. He had always said, "If I'm there, you won't have anything to worry about." Now it was time for him to prove it.

He asked what was going on, and I barely got the words out: "He's here."

Before I could say another word, he walked into the room.

I heard him shout, "What are you doing here? Didn't I tell you what I'd do if you came after her?" Then he called out to me: "Come get the kids out of here!"

I ran to grab my children.

Within seconds, the abuser bolted out the door—and never came back. I was overjoyed. But my body told a different story. I had a large burn across my forehead, likely from his clothing rubbing against me while he was choking me. My heart was racing, my nerves fried—but I was alive, and my babies were safe.

Right after that incident, I decided to relocate my children and myself to another state. My ex didn't want me to leave New York, but he understood.

We never got back together, but we stayed in close contact. He drove across state lines weekly to visit the kids. His love for them never changed—and neither did our friendship. He helped more than ever, covering tuition, groceries, rent—whatever I needed, he made sure we had it.

Life moved on. I made new friends and dipped into short-term relationships, more out of loneliness than love. I craved companionship, so when a close friend wanted to move out of his parents' house and I wanted someone around, we decided to move in together.

We were better friends than partners. We disagreed often, but he had a great connection with my children. He enjoyed doing things with them, and I admired that about him. We were compatible in family life, but emotionally, we were never in sync.

I confided in my ex about the relationship and leaned on him for advice. At the same time, the financial support I had relied on from him started to slow down. Understandably so. I was living with another man. It wasn't his responsibility anymore.

This new man had his issues, and I had mine, but he brought fun and lightness that I had never experienced in my previous relationship. We traveled, threw parties, and enjoyed life to the fullest. It felt like a breath of fresh air. But things shifted. He lost his job, and I became the sole breadwinner in the household. The bills began piling up, and I found myself calling my ex for help again. He always came through. I never told my boyfriend where the money came from. I just knew our needs were being met.

Despite having a good corporate job, I couldn't afford the lifestyle I had grown accustomed to.

Then came another blow: I got pregnant. I wasn't ready. Finances were tight, and my emotions were all over the place, but then it got worse. I was told the pregnancy was ectopic. My tube had ruptured. I was rushed into surgery to remove the tube and the baby. Then, I heard the words that wrecked me: "You'll likely never be able to have children again."

I wasn't planning on more children. But when the doctors said I probably couldn't have any, something shifted in me. Suddenly, I wanted it more than anything.

Isn't it strange how you don't think about something until it's taken off the table?

I couldn't stop thinking about becoming pregnant again. The desire consumed me. I prayed, I cried, I read The Bible. I tracked my ovulation schedule. I had sex constantly. I stood on my head. I tried everything. I even sought astrologers, trying to piece together hope from anywhere I could. My mind was spiraling. But my faith—my little mustard seed of faith—kept me pressing, and then it happened.

Six months later, I was pregnant. Against the odds, I conceived. The one-in-a-hundred chance had happened for me. I knew it wasn't luck—it was a miracle—a gift from GOD.

That moment was a turning point. I wasn't fully healed, but I started seeing glimpses of the woman I was becoming—stronger, wiser, more protective of her peace. My healing wasn't loud, but it was happening.

I realized rebuilding didn't mean perfection. It meant refusing to live in the ruins of my past. I started giving myself grace. I started celebrating progress, no matter how small. I began to believe that God didn't bring me this far just to leave me in a state of survival.

I had a new foundation, faith. With that, I kept going.

God is Enough

"For God hath not given us the spirit of fear; but of power, and of love, and of a sound mind." – 2 Timothy 1:7 (KJV)

There were days I felt like I was unraveling—gripped by fear, drowning in shame, desperate for the pain to end. But God reminded me: I wasn't made to live tormented. He gave me power to stand, love to heal, and the promise of a sound mind.

The enemy tried to convince me I was crazy. But God showed me—I was finally finding myself.

Are your thoughts trying to trap you in fear or failure? Say this out loud: God gave me a sound mind. You are not broken beyond repair. You are not too far gone. You are His, and that changes everything.

Chapter 8:
Finding My Faith

There comes a moment when you get tired of surviving on broken promises and false hope. A moment when something inside you—what little strength you have left—rises and says, no more. I had reached that place. I was done crying over people who weren't crying over me. I've stopped shrinking myself to be accepted and stopped enduring pain disguised as love. This chapter is the turning point where I finally began to recognize my worth and reclaim my power.

When I gave birth to my son, at about six weeks old, my son was diagnosed with sleep apnea. He stopped breathing while he slept, turning blue so quickly it terrified me. His dad did his best to breathe into his mouth while I called EMS. It felt like they took forever to come.

I screamed out the window for help and called my paternal grandfather for prayer. He was a prayer warrior—a man of great faith. I believed that if anyone could get a prayer through to God, it was him. Well, he *was*—until I built my relationship with God.

The ambulance finally arrived, and while riding to the hospital, my grandfather instructed me to lay hands on my son while he prayed over the phone. The EMS workers kept demanding that I hang up, but I ignored them. I needed God to intervene—and He did.

By the time we got to the hospital, the staff was already outside with medical equipment, waiting for my baby.

He stayed in the hospital for about a week before being discharged home with a sleep machine. Thankfully, he eventually outgrew that issue and began breathing and sleeping normally.

The company I worked for had closed, and we were laid off around June 2001. I didn't know how we would survive financially, so I started searching for a new job.

With four children, rent, a car note, and other expenses piling up, my severance and unemployment couldn't cover it all. So, I did what I thought was best—I called my ex-husband again.

When my son was just over a year old, I agreed to do a favor for a friend to make a few dollars. That decision would change everything. It led to one of the most devastating consequences of my life: I ended up being out of my children's lives for almost three years. That one moment became a massive turning point in my life.

I was arrested—my first time in trouble with the law—and sent straight to the Segregated Housing Unit, known as the SHU. There were no windows. The cell was pitch black. Inmates were only allowed out for one hour of "outside" time, which consisted of standing in an enclosed space with three walls. You couldn't see outside—only look up at the sky.

The intake process was humiliating. I was strip-searched in front of a female officer, made to bend over and cough to prove I wasn't hiding anything. I was allowed a shower, but there were no curtains—just exposed bars—so the officers walking by could see everything. I was devastated.

Through this whole situation, no one was listening to my side. I had no voice. I had no way to explain my innocence. But I cried out to God. I prayed so hard in that cell.

One particular aspect I prayed for was my children. They were now in the care of my ex-husband and my maternal grandmother. I didn't know how they were doing. Were they okay? Were they eating? Did they miss me? I couldn't write to them—I had no pen or paper. I couldn't call—I didn't know the process or my rights. I felt helpless.

Eventually, I was transferred out of the SHU and into the general population, and it was a nightmare. I was terrified. I had to learn how to survive in a whole new world. I wasn't a fighter, but I became one.

The fear was real in the general population. I barely slept. I'd keep watch at night, observing everything and everyone, especially those in my dorm. I was on constant alert, afraid of being attacked.

Family visits were rare. I felt isolated and alone. I was moved from one jail to another, experiencing things I never could have imagined.

One of the jails I was in was a male facility. The women were placed on a separate floor, but that didn't stop some of the guards from taking advantage of them. Some women were raped. Others gave in to the guards' demands in exchange for favors—extra phone calls, longer showers, better treatment.

I cried and prayed every single day. I started writing my prayers to God in a small composition notebook. I poured out everything—my fears, my regrets, my hopes. I didn't have much, but I had that notebook and The Word. I read The Bible as often as I could. I wasn't the best reader, and I didn't always understand what I was reading—but I kept reading.

I attended chapel services whenever I could. I cried during praise and worship. I cried during the sermons. I cried when the chaplain spoke about forgiveness and mercy. I cried because I needed those things, but didn't know if I deserved them.

Over time, something started to shift. I began to believe God was really with me. I started to think that my life could change. I began to feel that I could be free, not just from jail, but from the pain and patterns that led me there in the first place. I wanted to be whole.

God began to reveal things to me. I saw my life more clearly. I saw where I went wrong, where I compromised, where I kept trying to fix things my way instead of His way. I saw the pain I caused—

and the pain I was carrying, and that's where my healing began.

All of this was just the beginning. Healing didn't mean I had it all together—it meant I was finally honest enough to start. I had found my starting place, and that place was faith. Through faith, God began to restore my life.

Saying *enough is enough* didn't mean the pain stopped immediately. It meant I stopped letting it define me. I still had healing to do. I still had work to face. But now, I was choosing to fight for myself.

God never meant for me to live in cycles of abuse, shame, or silence. He created me for more, and I was finally ready to walk in that truth. No matter how hard it would be, I had taken the first step. I was choosing God. I was choosing myself.

God is Enough

> *"To appoint unto them that mourn in Zion, to give unto them beauty for ashes, the oil of joy for mourning, the garment of praise for the spirit of heaviness..." – Isaiah 61:3 (KJV)*

I didn't think restoration was possible. My life felt like a pile of shattered moments—too scattered, too broken to make sense of. But God didn't ask for perfection. He met me in the ashes and offered beauty. He took my mourning and gave me joy. Every time I thought I had reached the end, He gave me a reason to begin again.

His love gave me the strength to gather the broken pieces and believe they still had purpose.

Do you feel like your life is too messy to fix?

Take heart. God specializes in broken pieces. What appears to be the end to you is just the beginning of His masterpiece.

Chapter 9:
When Trauma Tries Again

There comes a time when you think you've made it through. After all the pain, all the prayers, and all the healing, you start to feel like the worst is behind you. You begin to breathe again, smile again, and hope again. That's where I was. But trauma doesn't always knock politely—it barges in, uninvited, at the moment you finally begin to feel safe.

By the time I was released in 2004, I had become a new person. I thought differently and saw things in a different light. I needed to be independent again. I felt I needed to focus on myself and my children, but I took that independence to a whole new level. I rushed to save money and get my children back home. I did not realize that those 28 months had changed them, too. Their lives were impacted. They had experienced trauma in the worst ways. All I knew was that I needed to do what I needed to, and I was on the right track.

I got an apartment and a car, and around two years after my release, my children were back home. I just knew I was a winner. I was home with my children, working, and free—so it was all good. Yet, I struggled once again and felt overwhelmed. This life was not the one I was used to, nor could I function comfortably, as I had encountered different experiences.

I should have taken the opportunity to get myself together first. I should have taken my children to counseling to support the traumatic experiences they had encountered. I should have thanked my family—especially my brothers—for caring for my children in my absence, but I did not. I did things my way, and those things were not a priority on my list.

My children were going to high school when I got them back. They all started to rebel. They told me through various encounters, incidents, and experiences that they believed I would have prevented much of what had happened if I had been there. Today, they are coming to find out that nothing happened by accident. We are living in God's perfect will, and they are part of His perfect will.

Yet, thinking back to when we were struggling together, my teenagers took me through the ringer. I worked more hours than I spent at home, which contributed to their acting out. I was unable to provide them with all the attention they deserved. They previously remembered going places, eating, and enjoying themselves with their mother. Yet, this was no longer the case, and I had no extra resources to make it happen.

I found myself going around this mountain again, which I had been around before. I was struggling to make ends meet and needed to make sacrifices to take care of my children. I found myself in familiar territory again; this time, I was not helping anyone or doing any favors for money. I was riding this one out alone.

Somehow, I began to reflect on my past again and mentally relived my youth in some of the same situations. I felt like people dropped the ball with me from an early age. Trauma was evident, abuse was blatant, poverty was noticeable—and never addressed—and this is what my children were encountering in their way. I should have come home and put them into treatment, but I didn't. They, too, experienced a rough life, but it was never at the forefront of my mind.

Reflecting on my history and raising my children, there was a lot of dysfunction starting early in my life. As a young girl, I needed interventions that were not noticeable. So, looking at my then-teenagers, I knew my children required interventions, but I had too much going on to dedicate the time necessary for the intervention. Instead, I thought they were just rebellious and needed counseling. At some point, they did—and I did, too. We both required interventions during our childhood. As I didn't have time or make time to get them what they needed, maybe that was the same truth as my parents.

From 2006 to 2016, we experienced a challenging period. I maintained successful employment, remained a responsible and successful member of society, and was a dedicated mother.

I realized once my children started to rebel (and I started working with children and dysfunctional families) that when family ties are broken, it takes a lot of healing to bring that family back together. Love is a significant factor, but time and commitment are also necessary. Families need a support group to function, be productive, and grow healthy.

Through my experience, I developed a deep compassion for families. Although I could not dedicate the time I needed for my own, I had compassion for families within my heart.

Being away, I had numerous discussions with women who had similar and worse stories than mine. They had no family and made their own in prison. Some had family, and, because of bridges being burned, poverty-stricken conditions, or other reasons, they were not able to see their children.

I did not see my children often during my time away either. Actually, I saw them once, and I think that did us more harm than good, only because I wanted to see them again and did not want them to leave, and they wanted the same thing.

Today, my children and I are in a better place and grateful for the change that has occurred.

My life included other changes as well. My boyfriend, the father of my last child, had understandably moved on and relocated to another state. My grandparents moved south as well. Even further, I stopped making friends only to have someone's shoulder to lean on, and I started leaning on GOD. Lastly, I began to speak to my brothers and sisters more often.

God delivered me out of my trouble (with jail time), which was absolutely a miracle—to come out with no scars or blemishes—but I will never experience that again. If that was a way for God to get my attention—and I believe it was—then He has it.

I believe God had to put me in a place where I was away from everything and everyone, allowing me to focus on Him. The Bible declares that His ways are not our ways and that His thoughts are higher than our thoughts (Isaiah 55:8-9). What the enemy had planned for bad, God turned it around for my good.

God is Enough

"He healeth the broken in heart, and bindeth up their wounds." – Psalm 147:3 (KJV)

There were wounds so deep that they became an integral part of how I functioned. I had learned how to survive without healing. But God doesn't just look at the surface; He goes to the root. Every layer of pain I tried to hide, He exposed with gentleness and healed with love. His hands didn't reopen wounds to shame me—they touched them to restore me. Slowly, I came to realize that even the most difficult parts of my story were still worthy of healing.

Are there layers of pain you've buried just to make it through the day? Let this be the moment you permit God to go deeper.

He doesn't hurt to harm—He touches to heal. Trust Him with your wounds.

Chapter 10:
God at Work—And It's Showing

After everything I had been through—the abuse, the heartbreak, the near losses—I started to see something shift. It wasn't just that life was getting better. It was that God was showing up in ways I could no longer deny. Doors were opening. Peace was entering, and joy—real joy—was returning. It didn't mean the battle was over, but I was beginning to see the evidence of God's hand on my life. And this time, I was ready to embrace it.

I became a proud grandmother in 2012. Around the same time, I returned to school to pursue a bachelor's degree in psychology, driven by my deep passion for helping families. My dream was to own my own business eventually. After completing that degree, I continued and earned my MBA.

My journey took a divine turn in 2011 when I met my spiritual mother. That same year, I had been laid off from my job working with children and families. I enrolled in a training program to become a substance abuse counselor and completed it. During this time, my spiritual mother and I began talking regularly. She is a God-fearing woman, and her encouragement and consistent urging for me to get on the prayer line made a lasting impact. I didn't realize it at the time, but God was using her as a vessel to guide me to the place He had prepared for me.

With all this change, I still felt a sense of emptiness. I didn't know exactly what I was searching for, but I knew I never wanted to relive the pain I had already been through. I shared my dreams and fears with my spiritual mother, and she reminded me often that God had grand plans for me. Her prayers—both with me and for me—sustained me at a time when I needed them most.

As I continued my walk with God, the year 2012 met me with several trials. First, my son was diagnosed with a critical illness and rushed to the ICU. Around the same time, my daughter was hospitalized due to postpartum depression. Emotionally and physically overwhelmed, I was constantly shuttling between hospitals while caring for my granddaughter. My then-boyfriend, now husband, supported me as much as he could—especially with helping care for my granddaughter—but I was stretched thin.

Eventually, I had to take time off from work and was laid off again. My son was gravely ill, diagnosed with type 1 diabetes. I hadn't realized how sick he was, even though he was right under my nose. He would crawl under me, and I just thought he was being clingy.

One day, one of my other sons said, "Mom, you should take Jr. to the doctor. He's sick or something—all he does is lie around and sleep." That comment struck a nerve. Suddenly, everything made sense—he was sluggish, constantly tired, and drinking lots of water. I rushed him to the ER, where they found his blood sugar was dangerously high—over 800. He was on the brink of death.

As machines surrounded him in the ER and he was rushed to the ICU, my mind flooded with guilt and fear. How did this happen? Was I not paying attention? Was I a bad mother? My thoughts spiraled, and I could feel myself slipping into depression again.

But I couldn't allow myself to stay there. I had a daughter in the hospital, a granddaughter depending on me, and now a hospitalized son. I stayed with him daily, often waiting until he fell asleep. I would try to be back early the next morning.

When my boyfriend got off work, he would watch my granddaughter so I could be with my son. At times, I even brought her with me to the hospital—against policy—but the nurses understood and allowed it.

The day my son was scheduled to be discharged, I was utterly depleted. His doctor could see the exhaustion all over my face. When I admitted I felt sick, she kindly but firmly told me to go home, rest, and return when I had the strength to care for him. I was deeply grateful for her compassion, and she remains his doctor to this day.

A week or two later, my daughter came home. Although still somewhat unstable, she was showing improvement. My granddaughter stayed with me in the meantime.

In the midst of it all, my son questioned God—and truthfully, so did I. He didn't understand why this had happened to him, and I didn't have all the answers. But I did have The Word of God. I reminded him that *"We are more than conquerors through Christ,"* and I held on to that for both of us.

Despite my outward display of faith, I struggled with guilt. I blamed myself for not seeing the signs. I had been so consumed with work and life that I overlooked how sick he was. He tried to express his discomfort, but I didn't catch it. That realization tormented me.

I turned to a book I had owned for some time but never opened—*Battlefield of the Mind* by Joyce Meyer. That book, at that moment, was exactly what I needed. Not just for the scriptures, but because it helped me face the mental warfare of guilt and neglect. It helped me begin healing from the inside out.

One scripture that anchored me was *Isaiah 40:31—"But they that wait upon The Lord shall renew their strength; they shall mount up with wings as eagles…"* It reminded me that I could rise again.

I also reflected on how this book, *Enough is Enough*. I remembered the revelation I received while sitting in a jail cell during a court case. God gave me the title and the charge to write. As I wrote, I gained strength, even though I had no clue how it would be published.

I just held on to God's promise in *Jeremiah 29:11*—that He had plans for my life.

As things began to settle down with the medical issues my children were facing, my relationship with my children began to fall apart. My oldest children started acting out again. I was prepared this time. I had a plan.

I began searching for a smaller apartment for myself and my two younger boys. I also got a separate apartment for my older children, covering the security deposit and first month's rent. They were young adults at the time—high school graduates just beginning to work—and I wanted to give them a fresh start. Unfortunately, they didn't keep up with the rent. That's another chapter entirely.

At the time, I thought their behavior was typical teenage rebellion. I didn't realize they were acting out from deep emotional pain. I reached out to other family members, hoping for help, but they, too, dismissed it as "normal teen stuff." Looking back, I see now that they were hurting, and many of the adults around them were too.

This message is for parents, guardians, and caretakers: We can't afford to assume. When we make uninformed assumptions, we risk dismissing cries for help. I'm not saying everything that happens is someone else's fault—but I am saying we must be educated, spiritually grounded, and intentional. God has provided us with tools and wisdom to help us raise our children, and we must utilize them.

If I could go back, I would have sought family therapy. I would've sat down with my children and created space for them to open up and heal. But now, I hold fast to this truth: generational curses are being broken through me, through my children, and my grandchildren. The enemy will not win.

God is Enough

"Many are the afflictions of the righteous: but The Lord delivereth him out of them all." – Psalm 34:19 (KJV)

I didn't think I'd need another rescue—I thought I had already survived the worst. But cycles have a way of circling back until we break them for good. When fear tried to settle in again, God intervened once more. He didn't grow tired of saving me. He didn't hesitate to respond. He reminded me that deliverance isn't a one-time gift—it's a promise. And every time I was trapped, He showed up as my way out.

Do you feel like you should be "past this by now"? Don't let shame talk you out of grace. God is not tired of rescuing you. When you cry out, He still answers. Let Him do it again.

Chapter 11:
A Work in Progress

There's a reason this chapter is titled *A Work in Progress*. Life doesn't become easy just because we believe. Healing, growth, and transformation are lifelong processes, and every chapter of my life has demonstrated this to me. But there's one thing I've learned for sure: real, intentional love matters.

We, as a people, must begin to love one another truly, for this is the will of God.

"Beloved, let us love one another: for love is of God; and every one that loveth is born of God, and knoweth God." – 1 John 4:7 (KJV)

Love isn't just a feeling—it's protection, shelter, compassion, and understanding, especially when we don't fully grasp what someone else is going through. Teenagers, for example, can be a handful—but they have stories too. Everyone does. That's why I challenge you to see people through different lenses before making judgments. Had love been present in my own life—real, stable, healing love—some things might have turned out differently. I believe God's will still shaped my experiences, but I also know that love could have softened the journey.

Around 2018, things started to shift for me again. I was blessed with a new car and moved into a better neighborhood where my son could attend a quality school. I didn't have much financially, but I held onto the belief that God was making a way for me. I stayed content and kept praying, trusting that the battle was already won.

In that season of blessing, I hit a wall, both physically and emotionally. I was tired, exhausted. "Enough is enough," I said to God.

I clung to this Scripture: *"I am come that they might have life, and that they might have it more abundantly." – John 10:10 (KJV)*

I made a sincere request: Lord, don't let me leave this earth without experiencing that abundant life You promised. That prayer gave me strength because it aligned with His Word. If He said it, why shouldn't I believe it?

I used to tell my children, "If you go to college, I'll do everything I can so you can focus on school." In the same way, God asks us for our obedience and worship, and then takes care of the rest.

Still, something wasn't sitting right. Even with the new car, a better home, and a better district for my son, I still felt stagnant.

I couldn't afford a vacation or simple treats. I felt like I was always robbing Peter to pay Paul. Maybe I was living beyond my means? But I knew in my soul I wasn't created to struggle like this.

"Take therefore no thought for the morrow: for the morrow shall take thought for the things of itself..."
– Matthew 6:34 (KJV)

That verse used to comfort me, but I couldn't help but think—how does it apply when you have nothing for tomorrow?

I wrestled with so many thoughts. The Scripture says, *"The just shall live by faith."* But I wasn't quite there yet. As I reflected on this and other scriptures, something stirred in my spirit. I had a yearning, a hunger, and a desire to grow closer to God. So I picked up my Bible.

One page at a time, I started reading. I began in Genesis, determined to let The Word of God live in me. I didn't always understand what I read, but I kept going. I prayed, "Lord, help me understand this so I can give it back to You when life doesn't look like Your promises."

One Sunday, my pastor preached a message titled "How to Live a Life That Wins," based on the book of Joshua. One Scripture that stuck with me was *"This book of the law shall not depart out of thy mouth; but thou shalt meditate therein day and night... for then thou shalt make thy way prosperous, and then thou shalt have good success."* – Joshua 1:8 (KJV)

"If meditating on God's Word is all it takes, why not try?" is what I thought.

For the next few months, I prayed, read, and consecrated myself. But peace still didn't come easily. I was now married, in a new place, with a new car—but I was restless.

Then the attacks began again—this time at work.

My manager and supervisor began to give me a hard time. It felt like my coworkers didn't like me either. I was doing my job and praying for an open door, but nothing was happening yet. The company was acquired, layoffs hit, and responsibilities were shuffled. I didn't get a raise, but I did gain new skills in the process.

To help make ends meet, I started selling insurance part-time. That's when things got worse. Some coworkers falsely accused me of using company resources for personal business. I was called into an HR meeting. I was angry—not just because it wasn't true, but because my manager believed them.

Then she told me I seemed uninterested and my performance was slipping.

Maybe I was slipping. Perhaps the weight of everything was starting to take its toll. But that meeting lit a fire in me. I snapped back into gear. I couldn't afford to lose my job—not now. I went to God in prayer and begged Him for direction. I was finally starting to build a relationship with Him, and I wanted to trust Him in everything.

Just two weeks later, our site was downsized. They needed someone to lead the new remote location—

and to my surprise, the same manager who had reported me to HR chose me for the job.

I was shocked but grateful. I knew it was God.

The new role came with leadership responsibilities, a company phone, and occasional remote work. It was hard—I worked long hours and often brought tasks home—but I sensed that God was positioning me for something greater.

About six months to a year later, that new manager resigned, leadership changed again, but my role and pay stayed the same. Then, I needed surgery and had to take a medical leave. While recovering, I promised myself: when I go back, I'm going after something better, and that's exactly what I did.

Before returning, I was hired at a new company. From the very beginning, I knew God was up to something. I showed up to work as if I were working for The Lord, not for man. I served as if I were expecting a promotion. Even when I was tempted to snap back or be sarcastic, I bit my tongue. I had something to prove—to God and myself.

I was transparent during the interview process. I told them I wanted leadership. The hiring manager explained that new departments were being developed and that if I performed well, I'd be considered.

I've always been known for being straightforward, and in the past, that hasn't always worked in my favor. I've lost friendships because of my mouth. But this time, I was determined to walk upright—to live for God. Even then, the tests came.

One day, while working in collections, a customer accused me of being rude. My supervisor, who sat right next to me and could hear everything, sent an email to our manager with a formal warning. I was crushed, primarily because that same day, I had just spoken to the manager about possibly becoming a team lead.

I went for a walk outside. Tears streamed down my face as I cried out to God. I knew that accusation wasn't true. I reminded Him of His promises.

Later, I pulled my supervisor aside. I told her the truth—that I had escalated the call to her because the customer became irate. She admitted she hadn't been paying attention. I could've let bitterness take over, but instead, I chose to trust God to vindicate me.

That night, I got into an argument with my husband over something small. It felt like the walls were caving in. Every direction I turned, it seemed like I was under attack. I remember asking, "God, where are You in all of this?"

The next morning, I wept the entire drive to work. I passed house after house in my neighborhood, pleading with God. I declared, "You said I'm the head and not the tail. Above only and not beneath. That I would lend and not borrow. That no good thing would You withhold from those who love You." I kept repeating scriptures, desperate to feel His presence. I didn't want to hear about miracles—I wanted to *live* one.

I cried, "God, I believe You. I'm turning to You now. Please turn to me."

When I pulled into the parking lot, my face and shirt were soaked. I ran to the bathroom to clean up and started my day as usual. Then something unexpected happened.

Without much thought, I picked up my phone and texted my former manager to see how she was doing. She responded instantly. She thanked me for reaching out and mentioned a snowstorm happening in the Carolinas. I hadn't even heard about it.

Out of nowhere, she said, "You're going to live a long time. I was just talking about you!" Then came the miracle. She told me her new company was opening a department near me, and they needed a supervisor. She had already recommended me.

I couldn't believe it.

She had shared my experience and work ethic with the hiring team. They were eager to meet me.

I went to my car and cried again—but this time, it wasn't desperation. It was *confirmation*. God had heard me. He showed up in a way I never expected. At the very moment I thought He was silent, He was already setting up a new door.

Now, I walk by faith with complete confidence that God is listening to me. That He sees. He moves. Even in seasons of silence, He's never still. No matter what comes next, I've made up my mind—I won't turn back.

God Is Enough

> *"And if it seem evil unto you to serve The Lord, choose you this day whom ye will serve... but as for me and my house, we will serve The Lord."* –
> Joshua 24:15 (KJV)

Life gave me options—painful ones, tempting ones, dead-end ones. I had seen what choosing people, pleasure, or pain got me. But when I finally decided on God, everything shifted.

It didn't mean life got perfect—it meant my heart got anchored. I stopped living for survival and started living for *purpose*.

Choosing God wasn't just a one-time moment; it was a daily decision to believe that He is the better way, every time.

What are you still choosing over God?

Be honest, not for guilt's sake, but for growth's sake. You can start fresh right here. Choose Him again, and watch how choosing God rewrites everything.

Chapter 12:
Choosing God

I didn't know it at the time, but the lessons I was learning in Chapter 11 of my life—about spiritual warfare, vindication, and God's faithfulness—were running parallel to the deeper work God was doing in my home, my marriage, and most importantly, in my heart. While I was crying out in my car and navigating attacks at work, I was also being transformed from the inside out.

This chapter is not a sequel to the last—it's the mirror. While God was shifting things publicly, He was also pruning things privately. I had won battles at work, but God was waging war for my soul at home, and the battleground was my obedience. Choosing God didn't start in the sanctuary. It began in the silence of my own choices.

It had been about 45 days since I left a toxic situation behind. As stated, I had a new job, a new car, and a better school for my son. From the outside, things seemed to be moving forward. But on the inside, I was navigating unfamiliar territory—one where the things I used to lean on were no longer enough to hold me.

I had a new respect for myself and others, but more than that, I had a growing reverence for God. My husband and I had worked through many of our issues—not because we solved them all, but because God began shifting my lens. My prayers weren't about fixing him anymore. They were about finding myself.

When my husband and I first met, our bond was formed through shared experiences—bars, clubs, weekend drinks, and late-night laughs. I wasn't a heavy drinker, and I hated how more than a glass made me feel, but those moments helped us escape, helped us connect. The tension between us always seemed to melt away after a few sips.

But as my relationship with God deepened, my appetite for those escapes faded. Slowly and quietly, The Spirit started removing my taste for things I once craved. It wasn't dramatic or sudden—it was subtle, sacred. I used to hear people say, "I just don't want to do those things anymore," and I doubted it. But now I was living it.

My husband and I began to shift out of rhythm. The things that once brought us close no longer served the same purpose for me. I stopped getting upset when he stayed out late. I started craving solitude, gospel music, and peace. At first, I worried he was leaving me behind, but the truth was—I was being led forward.

He hadn't changed. I had, and that came with consequences. Some of his frustrations weren't because he stopped loving me. It was because I was no longer the same woman he married. He didn't recognize this version of me, and honestly, I was still getting to know her, too.

Eventually, I began to expect things I had never required before—things like being spoken to with unwavering respect by me and my children. In the past, I let things slide. I laughed things off, minimized disrespect, and tolerated emotional distance. Why? Because I didn't fully respect myself. I was grateful just to be chosen. I clung to people with a wounded heart, thinking that proximity to love was the same as being loved.

However, as I grew in my faith, my standards rose in tandem with my healing. I didn't want to be controlled or managed—I wanted to be cherished, protected, and seen. My husband wasn't the only one experiencing a change. I was evolving from a woman surviving trauma to a woman learning to walk in truth. I was becoming whole.

I joined a Christian sorority during this time, and that process was life-changing. The assignments were challenging and uncomfortable. But they were necessary. They pushed me to confront not just what I believed about God, but what I thought about myself. That process birthed in me a woman of stature and faith. It didn't happen overnight, but something in me finally began to stand.

I went from lying flat on my stomach in despair to crawling. Spiritually speaking, I had movement again. I wasn't strong yet, but I was no longer still, and that alone was a miracle.

As I continued my relationship with The Lord, my husband began to feel even more distant and suspicious of my change. He questioned my motives. "You're only going to church because you want something from God," he once said. He wasn't wrong. I *did* want something. But it wasn't material. I wanted peace. I wanted wholeness. I wanted to feel safe inside myself for once. I wasn't chasing blessings—I was chasing The Healer.

Our relationship grew tense. At one point, we even discussed the possibility of separation. The emotional disconnection felt unbearable. We no longer recognized each other, and to be honest, I barely recognized myself. What used to upset me no longer does, and what didn't used to bother me now does. We were both grieving the version of me that was gone.

Still, I kept going. I didn't have all the answers, but I had a longing for God that wouldn't quit. I had a desire to grow, to heal, and to finally get free from the cycles that had trapped generations in my family. I was willing to walk alone if necessary.

I still had insecurities. I still struggled with confidence and confrontation. But I had something now that I didn't before: *hope*. That hope was lighting the way forward.

My children saw the change in me, even if they didn't always understand it. I was parenting differently—not perfectly, but intentionally. I wasn't trying to be their best friend. I was trying to give them something I never had: a mother with boundaries, love, and a vision. I still carried guilt for the pain they experienced growing up, for the chaos they didn't deserve, for dragging them through my storms. But I also knew this: the same God who was healing me could also heal them.

I released the pressure to fix them. Instead, I started interceding for them.

That's when the shift happened, not just in them, but in me. I started seeing them not just as my children, but as God's children too. I realized they had a purpose and process of their own, and my job was to pray, to model, and to release them into His hands.

I started building again—but this time, with purpose. I launched a podcast to help families like mine and wrote this book. I even began working on ministry initiatives to help women and children find identity and healing.

None of this was about becoming famous (and none of this continues to be about being famous). It was about becoming *faithful*.

My pain had a purpose. My scars had stories. And if someone else could be set free by hearing them, then I'd speak up—even if my voice trembled.

I didn't need a pulpit to preach. I just needed to live loudly enough that people could hear God through my healing.

Even now, I keep a quiet place in my life where I meet with Him. Sometimes, it's the car. Other times, it's the closet, the bathroom, or a walk. It's not always glamorous. Most of the time, it's not even pretty. But it's real. It's raw, and it's where I've grown the most.

There, I've learned that obedience matters more than opinions. That healing is not just for me. It's for generations. I also learned that God never wastes a wound.

I still fall short. I still have days where old habits creep up, where insecurities knock on the door, where I feel the tug of fear. But I don't live there anymore. I've moved, both spiritually and emotionally. When the enemy tries to drag me back, I know too much now. I've tasted freedom. I've chosen God, and I'll keep choosing Him—because I know what it looks like to live without Him.

God is Enough: Final Meditation

> *"But the God of all grace, who hath called us unto his eternal glory by Christ Jesus, after that ye have*

suffered a while, make you perfect, stablish, strengthen, settle you." — *1 Peter 5:10, KJV*

I have suffered. I have stumbled. I have screamed into pillows and sobbed in silence. I have been overlooked, abandoned, and misjudged. But the God of all grace picked me up, over and over again. He strengthened me. He settled me. He healed me, layer by layer.

This book is not just my testimony—it's my transformation.

I am no longer trying to convince others that I'm worthy. I know I am. I am no longer performing for love. I am rooted in it. I am no longer afraid of starting over—I've done it with God, and He's made all things new.

I say with boldness: God is enough for me.

For the Reader:

You've walked with me through the darkest valleys and brightest breakthroughs. You've seen my shame, my scars, my silence, and my surrender.

But this moment? This one is about you.

You are not alone. You are not disqualified. You are not too broken.

God is still writing your story. Your tears are not wasted. Your pain is not pointless. Your voice is needed, just like mine was.

Stand up. Speak your truth. Choose God fully and forever.

Do this immediately because enough is enough, and God is more than enough.

ABOUT THE AUTHOR

Marisa Mason

Author | Podcaster | Advocate for Healing & Purpose

Marisa Mason is a resilient voice of truth and transformation. As the author of *Enough is Enough* and the host of the "Intentionally BU Podcast," Marisa empowers women to rise above their past and live boldly in their purpose.

Born and raised in New Jersey, Marisa's early life was marked by trauma, abandonment, and deep personal loss—but it was also where she found her voice. Through adversity came resilience. Through pain, purpose. Her experiences with homelessness, domestic abuse, and family brokenness have become the foundation for the healing message she now shares with the world.

A devoted wife, mother, and grandmother, Marisa is equally passionate about faith, family, and freedom—freedom from shame, cycles of dysfunction, and the silent struggles so many carry. She holds an Associate's Degree, two Bachelor's Degrees, and a Master's Degree in Business

Management with a specialization in Public Administration.

Today, she uses her platform to speak truth with love, encourage those still in the fight, and lead others with grace into the healing they deserve. Through her writing, podcasting, and mentoring, Marisa reminds us that no matter where you've been, healing is possible—and the enemy doesn't get to write your ending.

STAY CONNECTED

Marisa Mason

I would love for you to stay connected with me as I continue my journey of ministry and writing. Follow, engage, and keep in touch through the following platforms:

Website: Visit my official website for updates on upcoming books, events, and more:

IntentionallyBU.com

Email: For personal inquiries, prayer requests, or updates, reach out via email:

marisamason71@yahoo.com

Social Media: Connect with me on social media for daily inspiration, insights, and up-coming events:

- **Facebook:** IntentionallyBUPodcast
- **Instagram:** IntentionallyBUPodcast

THANK YOU FOR READING!

I hope this book has brought you joy, inspired you, and positively impacted your life. Your feedback is essential, and I'd love to hear from you!

Leave a Review and 5-Star Rating

How to Leave a Review on Amazon

1. Go to the book's page on **Amazon** (search for the title or author).
2. Scroll down to the **Customer Reviews** section.
3. Click on **"Write a Customer Review."**
4. Select the number of stars and write your feedback.
5. Click **Submit**—and that's it!

Thank you for being so supportive. Your feedback can help others find this book and experience the same impact.

May GOD continue to bless and guide you on your journey.

www.ingramcontent.com/pod-product-compliance
Lightning Source LLC
Chambersburg PA
CBHW050644160426
43194CB00010B/1805